Travel Souvenirs

haiku from near and far

Adelaide B. Shaw

ISBN: 978-81-948271-3-9

First Edition: 2020
Rs. 200/-

Cyberwit.net
HIG 45 Kaushambi Kunj, Kalindipuram
Allahabad - 211011 (U.P.) India
http://www.cyberwit.net
Tel: +(91) 9415091004 +(91) (532) 2552257
E-mail: info@cyberwit.net

Printed at Repro India Limited.

The journey itself is my home.

Matsuo Basho

The real voyage of discovery consists not in seeking new land-scapes, but having new eyes.

Marcel Proust

My souvenirs are not tangible objects, but happenings recreated in words and stored in memory.

Adelaide B. Shaw

Acknowledgements

I wish to thank the editors of the following journals for publishing some of these haiku and senryu, either as they appear here or in an earlier version:

A Hundred Gourds, Bottle Rockets, Contemporary Haibun Online, Dragonfly, Frogpond, Gean, Green's Journal, Haibun Today, Haigaonline, Haiku Highlights, Hoi Polloi, Lynx, Modern Haiku, Nisqually Delta Review, Presence, Shamrock, Simply Haiku, Simply Stylus Journal, World Haiku Review, Yellow Moon.

Preface

During my lifetime, I have been fortunate to have traveled to and lived in many places, staying in some for only two days, in others, much longer. This collection of haiku and senryu does not include all that I saw and wrote. These poems are some of the images, impressions and memories. Changes occur over time, and what I wrote about ten, twenty, thirty years ago and more, may not be true now.

Los Angeles, California and Environs

1952-2019

When I was sixteen, I moved with my parents and sister from New Haven, Connecticut, my birthplace, to Los Angeles. I left in 1971 with my husband and three children, but have visited several times since then.

new school
new sensations
tacos and smog

oversized billboards
tinsel town
in your face

movie stars' homes
get close and personal
with dots on a map

surfs up!
Newton's law proven
with a splash

pre-dawn quake
shaking us out of bed
to view the sunrise

water gurgles
over slippery rocks
losing myself

squiggling tide pools
a small finger
goes in and out

dry roasted hills
sprinkled with sage
the powdered dust

late afternoon
fire in the canyons blazing
in the sea and sky

in the high valleys
breathing the virgin air
pine scent on my hands

Mission landmarks
we follow the fragrance
of eucalyptus.

doves cry
behind the white-washed church,
“You’re a fool, you’re a fool”

in the dark doorway,
eyes shut at the white sand—
a stabbing light

a power saw
breaking the three o’clock silence
the day moves on

earth shaking news:
the LA skyline
tall and taller

the old neighborhood
in a time capsule—
jacaranda May

Hollywood Boulevard
forward *"unto the breech"*
to shoot a selfie

coming home
still the snow-capped hills
and sunshine poppies

England

November, 1971

My husband accepted a position with the United Nations in Geneva, Switzerland. On the way to Geneva, we made an overnight stop-over to help us adjust to the time change.

London Arrival

a jet lag tour
through coal smoke and fog
the bells of Big Ben

Madame Tussaud's
the waxy-eyed look
when leaving

deep descent. . . deeper
into the underground
recalling Dante

ploughman's lunch
with a second ale
the afternoon's gone

Switzerland

1971-1976

During our stay in Switzerland, we lived in the small village of Gland, about twenty miles north of Geneva.

Arrival In Geneva

gray on gray
the porter's puzzled look
at my high school French

hotel breakfast
the warming sounds of coffee
being poured

dinner at midnight
real time
and body time

string bag bulging
shop to shop learning
the currency

Village Life

newly seeded field
a gathering of crows
pecking and cawing

dawn blessing of cows
plodding the way up
to summer pastures

long ago stories
above lush meadows
a wooden hut

napping in clover
sharing the sweetness
with bees

early morning walk...
a stop for buttercups
the bread forgotten

turning the rich earth
a farmer watches gulls
circling the field

ramble in the woods
the wild fragrance
of mushrooms

rolling green hills—
here and there a cement bunker
entangled with vines

construction debris
free for the taking
red poppies

the scent of wild mint...
remembering too late
the spiny leaves

night life
the café's German Shepard
snaps at flies

Christmas In Gland

oranges or coal
a skinny Kris Kringle
reaches in his bag

village decorations—
snow covered fields
under moonlight

midnight Mass
the small wooden church bursting
with song

A Day In The Jura

layers of mountains
fused with mist…
the cloud peaks

flower splashes
spilling out of windows
filling the gardens

stone houses
crumbling walls patched
with geraniums

plot, plop on the road…
cars follow the cow trail
to the milking barn

an open barn
the odor of hay and manure
and climbing roses

summer tourists
walking the ski runs
the easy swiftness

late day sunshine
wheat and corn fields
checkerboarding the hills

On The Way To Fribourg

picnic in a grove
sitting on rocks
the seeping dampness

looking for sky,
seeing only mossy trunks
and wild ivy

gathering berries
the plink, plink. . .plink
then silence

the squish of red leaves—
slowly our talking. . .
stops

A Night In The Simplon Pass

the high peaks—
swirling clouds
leaving snow behind

the swish of tires
and the click, click of wipers
in quickening snow

stuck in a snow bank
three languages
babbling help

only the snow
reflected in the car's beams
the village lights

thick down quilts
drifting into sleep
on waves of wind

When my parents and niece visited, we had to have a larger vehicle for traveling.

Zurich

rented VW bus
four children ask
"Are we there yet?"

a sick child
the day begins at dawn
with clean sheets

another patient
the concierge no longer smiles
when bringing towels

guardian angels
Grandpa and Grandma wing it
with survivors

hubby laid low
another day to explore
my hotel room

Zurich souvenir
Nurse Nightingale wears
a loden green folk dress

Italy

February, 1972

Our first trip to Italy was a two-hour drive south and east of Geneva.

Aosta

land of my genes
familiarity
in the faces

seeing my nonna*
the stooped old woman
with a distant smile

swaggering young men
stories
my father told

crinkly faced old men
drinking espresso—
those who stayed behind

rugged hills
a slender girl with a goat
scrabbling through time

*nonna: grandmother

April, 1972

The plan was to see friends in Rome, then drive on to Naples, which we had to cancel.

The Crash at Grosetto

Easter green—
meeting a lone tree
head on

jangling bells
goats scrambling down hill
first on the scene

hot cocoa for five
the signora continues
making pasta

stepping into
the wailing ambulance
offers of cake

dark hospital halls
the smell of alcohol
and . . .hardship

slow train to Rome—
at each stop the tired faces
of new passengers

Rome

Coliseum at dusk
the hungry eyes of cats
in the arena

Trevi Fountain—
jostling for space
in which to dream

morning espresso
Via Veneto
slowly comes awake

a temple . . . a church
the one clear light
in the Pantheon

the Catacombs
cold tunnels stacked with bones—
the disconnect

France

1971-1976

On weekends, we sometimes took day trips into France.

Mouthe

Sunday—
chickens scratching in the road
the flying dust

day of prayer
the murmuring river
at the grist mill

moss-covered church—
creeping through the open door
the warmth of May

in the graveyard
one freshly weeded patch
the sharp lettering

Annecy

rippling rainbows
along the canal
pastel houses

island castle—
more than
once upon a time

gentle breezes
from lavender to purple
dappled flowers

a narrow path—
stone houses
veiled with ivy

Chamonix

dark pines
flanking the white slopes
topped off with fog

the fading mist
ski runs
getting longer

afternoon sun
the thrill of speeding downhill
from a lounge chair

browsing the shops
another souvenir
of where I didn't ski

going home
the skiers sleep
in a twilight fog

August, 1972

My visiting parents took a train, while my husband and I, our children and niece, drove.

Paris

Avenue Foch
long reaching shadows
from number 84*

peaches
from a street vendor
ripe with worms

doors open to spring
perfuming Champs-Élysées
morning coffee

*84 Avenue Foch: the main Gestapo headquarters during the German occupation

Tuileries walk
the comfort
of a shady chair

late at night
a symphony
of taxi horns

the Eifel Tower
looking up, creaking sounds
in my neck

Spain

July, 1973

Splashing Down The Costa del Sol

hot pebbly beach
splashing away the grime
in a tepid sea

cannon ball jump
in the parador* pool
riding the waves

sun glare
the many shades of white
in white sand

small fishing village
a briny fragrance
in the sheets

*Parador: specially classified
hotels with historic or natural interest

Estepa

the brown hills—
white stucco houses anchored
with olive trees

siesta
our footsteps seeming louder
the further we walk

the hot shade—
eating bread and oranges
and red dust

Granada

hotel terrace
relief from the Spanish sun
in a gin tonic

lingering lovers
after midnight
a lone guitarist

bubbling water
in the Generalife Garden
step after step

filigree shadows—
arched doorways lead
to more shadows

heat tired—
at a cantina
tepid beer

wandering. . .
paella and flamenco
down a shaded alley

spices on my tongue
a cooling siesta
under a slow fan

red hibiscus
tucked behind my ear-
in love again

Murcia

cathedral walls
old women in black
finger their rosaries

afternoon stillness
stirring the air
with a tattered fan

the plaza at dusk
families gather
with supper in bags

strumming guitarist—
sweat down his face
as fingers fly

midnight
moonlight and mystery
reclaim the plaza

Siesta In Seville

the Giralda tower,
shimmering in the heat—
the empty streets

chinks of light
slipping through slatted blinds—
click of the fan

sweat beads up—
thinking of Marabella
and cool waters

sliding an ice cube
around my neck and shoulders
waiting for dusk

Algeciras

port stroll
fragranting the air
oil tankers and freighters

eyes on the ships
a missed opportunity
to see the curb

farmacia
the same anywhere
a pair of crutches

swelling ferry crowds
a swollen ankle
gets first in line

Morocco

July, 1973

The Casbah In Tangiers

imagining
veils and tambourines
sounds of rock and roll

twelve -year old guide
pushing. . .pushing. . .
promises of mint tea

culture and kitsch
serious bargaining
for a leather hassock

weaving through crowds
to the top of the Casbah
the desert winds

toothless snake charmer
a mottled cobra
coiled in a basket

not quite asleep
the cobra watching
through black slits

slow serpent spiral
rising. . . rising
to the waving punji*

our boy guide
looking cool in his long robe
hand out for a tip

*punji: a flute-like instrument

Italy and Austria

September, 1975

We traveled with visiting family and rented a VW bus again to accommodate five adults and four children.

VENICE

puddles in St. Mark's
tourists walking with eyes
looking up

pigeons
flying across the stones—
the Angelus bell

coffee and pastries
under the arches
a ringside seat

rain on the cobbles—
the arcade musicians pause
for more espresso

second floor window
church spires float
on bands of fog

the splash of oars
slipping through the mist
the gondola's lantern

wrap-around fog
swirling cognac
between sips

floating under
the Bridge of Signs
married lovers hold hands

Venetian glass
the maker's breath
shaping his heritage

After a week in Venice, we moved on.

Vienna

four kids studying
the border guard asks,
"Is this a school bus?"

glitter and glitz
in the Schönbrunn Palace—
exit to a blue sky

Vienna dancing
Lipizzaner horses
at the Riding School

tram ride
twice around the Ringstrasse
not enough

smoky café
the mid-morning rustle
as newspapers turn

Salzburg

exit from the bus
the hills are alive
with children singing

Mexican café
sizzling memories
of California

the hilltop fort—
sufficient for the day
strolling the outside

England, Belgium and France

After my husband transferred to the United Nations in New York in 1976, I sometimes accompanied him when he traveled.

August,1980

Cambridge

lazy on the Cam
the list of things to see
slips from my hand

the Bridge of Sighs
stone, spires, river, sky
in agreement

King's College Chapel
gliding on a breeze
a choir of birds

November, 1983

Thanksgiving In Brussels

chocolate
in the Grand Place
pigeons on parade

at the fish market,
mussels and *Mort Subite**
a meal to die for

pop music—
unintelligible words
French or English

*Mort Subite: A Belgium beer
meaning sudden death

smoky café—
settling near the window
a few dried leaves

creaky paddle fan
stirring the lace curtains—
flurries at dusk

in from the cold
he orders brandy for two-—
a Thanksgiving toast

December, 1983

Paris

a casual stroll
going wherever
the breezes go

Michelin book closed
the night lights of Paris
as our guide

the opera house
a top performance
by the Chagall ceiling

Dominica

January, 1986

For our twenty-fifth anniversary we went to Dominica, a quieter, less touristy island in the Caribbean.

puddle jumping*
to reach the island
regretting lunch

rolling thunderheads—
flying into the black sky,
eyes shut

humid heat—
bouncing on rutted mud roads
the island rhythm

wheels hugging a ditch—
poinsettias,
within reach

*short airplane trips,
usually in small planes

room with a view
a lullaby sung
in waves

island of rainbows
girls in pastel gingham
working in shops

cold grapefruit juice
morning wakeup or cocktail
rum optional

dread locks
and machete. . .
a smile and a wave

one whack
splitting the coconut–
gleaming white teeth

afternoon rainbow
the music
of dripping trees

rain forest
slowing down
for each snap and swish

the Emerald Pool
losing all words
in the falls

Mardi Gras Party
in the midst of revelers
dancing cheek to cheek

departure day
waiting out the showers
with a cold beer

The Arab Emirates

September, 1993

Dubai

luxury beach hotel
the long stretch of burning sand
before the Gulf

mud brick house
down the wind tower a breeze
sweeps the dirt floor

in the souk
the cool feel of gold—
ninety-eight in the shade

another journey—
sailing at sunset
a dhow*leaves the creek

*dhow: traditional Arabic sailing vessel

The Seychelle Islands

September, 1993

Mahé

a salamander
green against the pink wall
waiting…

inside, outside,
cacophony of languages
the voices of insects

trade winds
through the local bazaar
looking for a fan

power outage
stilling our chatter
the luminous waves

scented darkness—
the waitress serves
spicy curry

Praslin

eye to eye
with a tortoise on the road—
we drive the verge

an egret bobs
across the open lounge
rustling palm fronds

clear blue water—
refracted sunlight scatters
with each step

bikinied bathers
polished and on display
cocoa-de-mere*

*The cocoa-de-mere nut is a protected species of palm tree nut, the shape of which, when dried and polished, resembles buttocks. They are about 40-50 cm in diameter. (approx.16-20 inches)

La Digue

another souvenir—
biking on a dirt road
gravel in my knee

an empty cove—
footprints in the sand
ending at the water

lumbering oxen cart
the talkative driver
knows everyone

still standing
just a chimney
girded with vines

Portugal

October, 1993

Lisbon

Castelo de São Jorge
glinting in the sunshine
escudos* in my hand

pension on a hill
peasants and kings
the same view

sugary pastry
sticking
to the ribs

blue and yellow tiles
the sidewalk ends
in dirt and gravel

*escudos: Portuguese currency
before the Euro

downhill tram
a swing left, a swing right
exit laughing

endurance—
up and down, up and down
narrow streets

fado* from an alley
lingering sorrows
in her voice

autumn sunset
flaming the sky
second glass of port

*fado: songs of melancholy and sadness

Greece

May, 1997

Naxos

an inch of soil
between cobblestones
red geraniums

drooping
in the heat of midday
bougainvillea

sun-tanned limbs
lying on the hot sand
another goddess

lazy waves
the same shade of blue
where sea meets sky

blue and white bowl
holding ancient history
in my hands

embracing
the setting sun
the Portara Arch

moonlight and ripples
we share
a glass of ouzo

pink oleander
framing a blue door—
postcards for sale

The Hillside Towns

swaying bus
on a twisty rising road
views of the drop

Sunday afternoon
closed church doors,
open cafes

the dusty road—
a splash of red poppies
in the gravel

the hot wind—
a white stucco church
in the olive grove

uphill road
jingling goat bells
falling behind

cascading flowers
the smooth slide
of a cold beer

A Night In The Kastro

pushing our shadows
through narrow passages
unfamiliar angles

flickering lamplight
across the path
two cats on the run

sitting between
darkness and moonlight
a man with a pipe

twisting streets
in and out of moonlight
new contours

the warm night—
holding onto rough walls
cool to the touch

a woman's laugh
rises from a street below
never to meet

Turkey

May 1997

Istanbul

dawn
piercing the darkness
first call to prayer

roof garden—
through swaying trees
four, five. . .eight minarets

the old bazaar
streets of coffee and spice. . .
garbage in corners

cloaked women
shopping for bargains
bare-armed tourists

Istanbul
moving. . .moving
the hours between prayer

Istiklal Caddesi*
a girl with lowered eyes
holds up a comb

the Hippodrome
thundering horses
thundering crowds

boys fishing
from the Bosporus Bridge—
lunch undecided

low sunshine
apple tea from a vendor
a shade of amber

*the main shopping street in Istanbul

grandeur and splendor
in the Topkapi Palace
all that is not seen

jasmine scented secrets
wafting through corridors
in the harem

converted prison
climbing roses
on the iron gate

the Para Palace bar
drinking up legends
of spies and writers

an outdoor café—
sinking into soft cushions
eyes on the stars

Sultan Amet Cami

the blue mosque
grayness melding
into blackness

twenty thousand tiles—
dust motes swirl
in the blue light

women praying
behind the grills
averted eyes

sunset—
the muezzin's call
reaches the roof tops

wheeling gulls
in the lights of the mosque
the flash of wings

Ireland

September, 2010

Dublin

on and off rain
black umbrellas dipping
down and up

a soft day*
settling in a wing chair
for tea and scones

tour with a pint
at the Guinness Gravity Bar
I lose mine

Sunday church bells—
wrapped against the drizzle
a homeless man sleeps

* a soft day: In Ireland, a day of mist and fog

street mimes—
in the slanting sun
the bronze statue blinks

street fiddler
between tapping feet
pigeons strut the cobbles

wind off the river
clowns at the block party
swaying on stilts

second floor window
soaring with gulls
over the Liffey

Guinness Day*
the streets flowing
with free pints

Ha'penny Bridge—
crossing the Liffey
no toll for gulls

Dublin bustle
a girl and her dog
begging for breakfast

farewell sunshine—
the last walk through Dublin
wind at our back

* Guinness Day: Annual event to celebrate the founder, Sir Arthur Guinness. It was cancelled in 2014.

Galway

swans in Claddagh
stretching their necks
for the same hand-out

red sails flapping
a beached hooker*
pulls at the ropes

lights on the quay
with no moon
a brighter green

midnight revelers
Celtic songs usher in
a new day

first coffee
sipping the grayness
from the day

*hooker: fishing boat

On The Road

Ross Errilly Friary—
ancient prayers recited
in the wind

rock walls
here and there a garden,
a graveyard

Cong village*
The Quiet Man comes alive
each day at the pub

* the village where parts of the film were shot.

narrow road
wild shrubs slashing
at the bus

six-foot cairn
whistling winds keep company
with the dead

hills of grikes and clints*
cows grazing below
in green pastures

*grikes: the cracks between flat slabs of stone
clints: isolated slabs of stone

Connemara

County Galway

peat bogs
meeting in a pool
runnels of rain

against the wind
the squish and squelch
on hummocky hills

killer sheep*
rock over rock
my mincing steps

*black-faced sheep with curved horns

carrots ready
the gray mare and black colt
cease nuzzling

Kylemore Abbey
cloaked in mist—
the gardens up close

peat smoke
from the gardener's cottage–
turning back

Cliffs of Moher
County Clare

ribbons of fog
obscuring…revealing . . .
reshaping

sandstone and shale
the many layers
of legends and myths

shifting clouds
in the sequence of a breath
the mist clears

waves and wind
chiseling the Cliffs
now…and now…

a gull's flight
the speed in which lives
come and go

sea stack
the sculptor's hand
works slowly

Inish Mor

The Aran Islands

autumn equinox
huddling against the wind
on the ferry's deck

the tourist bit
after two weeks light baggage
gets heavy

the old man's song
from the pony trap
a slow clip-clop

roadside cross—
lost at sea or to the new world
the same prayers

wild blackberries
on rock boundaries
bitter fruit

church ruins
in the rubble the stone alter
standing solid

Dún Aonghasa*
a pause to measure
distance and strength

craggy hills and sea–
the village at sunset
folding for the night

*Dún Aonghasa: a prehistoric fort on
a cliff above the Atlantic in Kilmurvey

United States

October, 1983

Massachusetts

Nantucket

the sun not yet warm
watching the white caps
cold against the bow

a mid-week sail
solitary in the bay
one buoy light blinking

sea gulls squabble
on an empty stretch of beach
the colorless sand...

cobblestone streets
in the early darkness
clattering footsteps

end of season...
brown leaves
filling doorways

coffee and sunrise
on the return ferry
mind adjustment

August, 1985

Cape Cod

rental cottage
a quiet companionship
with a rabbit

floating mist
the lighthouse appears
in bits and pieces

slipping into the sea
one cold step
after another

spring evening
the dirt road stretches
to the day's end

a country night—
slowly the fog
wraps me inside

South Carolina

May, 2001

Charleston

cobblestone lane
English gardens
with palm trees

adjusting to the light
houses with double staircases
double balconies

Boone Plantation
the main house standing tall
above slave cabins

algae on the black pond
breaking apart—
emerging turtle

St. Helena Island

crumbling tabby* walls
magnolia branches
for the church roof

Spanish moss
from one live oak
to another

graveyard
the family names
sunken in the ground

*tabby: a type of concrete using oyster
shells, along with other materials

Georgia

May, 2001

Savannah

jasmine scented nights
slowing down
to the Southern pulse

dinner
and hot music—
low country boil*

Columbia Square
blending wrought iron
and flowers

horse carriage ride
nodding
to a slow clip-clop

*A boiled one pot meal of potatoes,
sausage, corn, onions and shrimp

Summer 2005

New York City

subway descent
a bobbing fern
ahead of me

shielding my eyes
from the sun glare—
a dash between cars

six dogs on a walk
in a tugging frenzy—
a leaf in their sights

fashionistas
on Fifth Avenue
the skinny is tweed

upper East side
a doorman and pigeons
come with the rent

ticket machine
choking on coins
spits nothing back

Upstate New York

2006 - 2019

Life in the Country

outdoor market
the farmer tells me
what to buy

autumn ritual
crowding the apple orchard
city day trippers

poison ivy
in between rows
bargain apples

after lunch
lazy in the sun
yellow jackets

roadside stand—
rolling over each other
pumpkins and people

up and down the hills
cawing and pecking
black dots on brown

fern glen
a pond, a frog, a splash
rippling

the cries of geese
crossing the hunting grounds
of ancient tribes

tire tracks on snow
around the farm's fences
last check before bed

damp morning
carried on the wind
fresh manure

thunder storm
leaves on the pond
regroup

journey's end
a country road
curving nowhere

silver frost meadows—
the swift passing
of a dew-drop morning

meandering stroll
we take the lane
with wildflowers

Millbrook

Sunday afternoon
the small town quiet
of Main Street

diner breakfast
ignoring the bitter cold
for a waffle fix

heavy coffee mug
the chips and scratches
of generations

church carnival
from two blocks away
squeals and laughter

Memorial Day
watching people
watching the parade

sudden breeze
goose pumps on my arm
when the pipers play

homecoming
the midnight owl returns
to the twin pines

storm warnings
we step into
our survival mode

Saturday in May
half the village
at the nursery

Florida

May, 2019

St. Augustine

The Robber Barons
gilt edged legacies
with some tarnish

heat stupor
the alligator's tail
slaps the water's edge

red stone fountain
the shimmer and sheen
of penny wishes

gecko spotting
a quick retreat
into the agave

scented night
a possibility
down every path

mottled sunshine
the flash
of a gator's teeth

spiced tea
southern breezes
in my cup

Spanish moss
silver spangles
under a full moon